Red Thread

Red Thread

poems

Teresa Mei Chuc

2012 · FITHIAN PRESS, McKINLEYVILLE, CALIFORNIA

Published by Fithian Press
A division of Daniel and Daniel, Publishers, Inc.
Post Office Box 2790
McKinleyville, CA 95519
www.danielpublishing.com

Cover painting *Blue Layers* by Ann Phong, artist, art instructor at Cal Poly Pomona
University, http://annphongart.com

Distributed by SCB Distributors (800) 729-6423

LIBRARY OF CONGRESS CATALOGING-IN-PUBLICATION DATA
Chuc, Teresa Mei.
 Red thread : poems / by Teresa Mei Chuc.
   p. cm.
 ISBN 978-1-56474-528-6 (pbk. : alk. paper)
 I. Title.
 PS3604.O9393R43 2013
 811'.6--dc23
                2011045743

For Alexander, Nikolai, Kainani
and for Earl J. McGillen

"The sky has nothing
why does it comfort me…"
—Hai Zi

According to Chinese legend, an invisible red thread connects those who are destined to meet, regardless of time, place, or circumstance. The thread may stretch or tangle, but it will never break.

In addition, the red thread is a protection and blessing cord in Buddhist tradition. It keeps the wearer in the compassionate embrace of the bodhisattvas.

Contents

Cartography of Family

The Bomb Shelter

When bombs are exploding outside,
it means that there are implosions.

Vibrations travel through air and liquid.

My amniotic fluid is imprinted with airplanes
dropping bombs and screams and fire.

In the bomb shelter in Saigon,
my father teaches my two-year-old
brother French. *"Je m'appelle Chuc Nai Dat."*

"Je m'appelle...."

Not Worth a Bullet

A bullet is made of
copper or lead.
Gunpowder is
poured into the case.
The firing pin hits the
primer at the back of
the bullet which starts
the explosion. Altogether,
the bullet and the case are
typically about two inches in length
and weigh a few ounces.

My father said that
the Vietcongs
told him and the other
prisoners while in
"re-education" camp
that they were not worth a bullet.
They would work for the Vietcongs
and then die.

A bamboo tree is smooth, long
with roots that hold the earth
with the strong grip of green
knuckles and fingers.
They are used to build houses,
fences, etc.
A bamboo tree can weigh sixty pounds
or more and be twenty feet tall.

The prisoners were forced to
walk barefoot up the mountains
and carry bamboo back to the camp.

Due to the weight of the bamboo,
they were only able to carry one
at a time.

Immigration

It is October, when the winds of autumn blow strong in
the Pacific.

There are over two thousand of us, sardines,
barely human and starving. We sleep on the floor and
wash ourselves with seawater. People are sick.

When someone dies from sickness, s/he is wrapped
in a blanket and tossed overboard during a Buddhist
chant.

I was only two years old and cannot recollect the dying
next to me, nor can I recollect my constant coughing nor
can I recall seeing my mother's worried countenance as she
contemplated our future, how my constant crying made
her want to jump overboard.

Cockroaches

A proposal by someone to my mom
after the Vietnam War: *Why don't*
you sell your baby, you don't have
anything to eat?

A response by my four-year-old brother:
No, don't sell my sister! There are lots
of cockroaches for us to eat!

When I returned to the country
eighteen years later, I saw them—
large, brown shiny tanks on the wall,

evidence of my brother's love for me.

Welding

Bending down and narrowing her eyes,
she holds a torch and the stream of fire
shapes a silver thread into swirls.

A plastic shield protects her eyes
from sparks of flame in her hand.
The fire polishes a crystal into
the colors of a city where she was born—
how we leave pieces of ourselves like shards.

Vietnam Ghost Stories

Ghost-like beings roam,
carrying the bones of the dead,
their steps heavy with the weight
of fields and fields.
And the dead too—
stories Mother tells
of the ghost with a long tongue
that licks dishes at night.

Gong-gong, Por-por

$4 - \frac{X}{3} = 2$

X is for my maternal grandparents
stuck in Vietnam after the war.

XX is for a girl—my mom
who was adopted when she was a baby.

X is for no proof of relationship.
My grandparents never changed

my mom's last name to theirs, because
girls will lose their names anyway.

X marks the spot
where I last saw my grandparents

when I was two years old.
X is how their lives and mine crossed.

X times 3 = 18
the age when I saw

and held my grandma, Por-por, again.
18 was the approximate number

of minutes I had with her before
I had to leave the small closet

space in which she was forced to live
in Vietnam. X was how our arms embraced.

X = 6
6 = family.

X = Gong-gong, Por-Por
X is part of the equation.

X is the unknown.

Hut-yee

When I was little,
I was told not to sit
like a beggar, a hut-yee.

That is, with one knee
up to my chest

like those beggars
and rickshaw drivers
on the streets of Saigon.

So, I was taught to sit
the way people in the U.S.
sit with both legs on the floor
and their back straight—a
ninety-degree angle.

Sometimes I can cross one leg
over the other.

I am supposed to sit the way
I want to be in the future and
that is certainly not a beggar.

But I think something differently:
I can still sit with my knee up
to my chest and not beg.

Quantum Equation

I watch my mother as she puts two cups
of rice into a small pot,
pouring water in and out, washing.
Moving rice around with fingers
until murkiness of water is gone
and the rice is clean.

She places her hand, palm down, on jasmine.
If water covers the fingers and knuckles
and not the back of the hand,
then there is enough to cook the rice to a nice
consistency.

In the future, I will cook rice this way.

My grandma bangs a gong as she prays.
The gong is round as a rice bowl,
its emptiness holds the world.
I run my fingers round and round the edge
until it sounds and I feel energy between fingers
and metal, a ring that makes my body tremble.

A rice bowl is round as haircuts.

The wetness creates a transparency for measurement.

I raise the rice bowl to my lips, absent-mindedly
pressing its bottom to my face as I wait for the food to be done.

Rose

When I was little,
my mom use to tell me not to smell roses
because the small bugs would get into my nose.
I avoided sniffing roses into adulthood.

One day, I saw a beautiful bush of red and white
roses.

I leaned closer than my mom would have liked.
It happened quickly, without a thought, a waft
like honey.

I smelled again.

Then I was curious about the purple ones, the
orange ones, and the deep red ones.

Moon Festival

In the middle of the mooncakes are egg yolks
surrounded by a red bean paste where centuries ago notes were
    hidden
by the Chinese to pass along rebellion war plans
to overthrow the Mongols. My parents buy these cakes for us to
eat every year—it is a tradition.

Genghis Khan and his descendants ruled the vast lands of China.
The Mongolians did not eat moon cakes.
I taste the night sky under which the rebels gathered.
How they organized in the dark and the salted moon crumbles on
    my tongue.

A Story of Mother and Daughter

She holds the baby cradled in her arms,
perpendicular to her body.
At that point of intersection—
two hearts are one.

The girl's body grows—no longer able
to stay horizontal in her mother's arms.
The bodies—vertical and parallel,
never really touching, yet yearning towards each other.

Cartesian Product

The set of yellow people
is the intersection of the set
of people and the set of yellow things.
So, I am seeking to find
where these two trains collide,
both leaving nowhere, heading for the
intersection at an incalculable speed.

Hugging My Grandma

This is how it feels
to hold a peach tree. Not
the trunk of the tree,
but the branches.
The bees circle to get
pollen and nectar,
so in my arms
are bees and butterflies
and fragrance and the assurance
of fruits. The branches
full of leaves and blossoms
and me just holding them in my open arms.

Grandma (A Hologram)

In your physical absence,
the hologram of me
still contains you
like a cut leaf—
you are part of the light
scattered from me so that even
a tiny fragment, an eyelash,
still contains the whole of you.

Wired Swan
for my son

Born into wire fencing, gazing
at the penned-in sky.

Someone is always watching, tapping, tapped.
And there is a regimen to follow

that consists of standardized testing, of sitting
still from class to class to class.

Encapsulated swan:
Such is this world. There is the

weightlessness of water and reflections.
The stretching of pure white wings
into the lightness of air.

How they flap and flap and flap
until the entire body presses upon barbs.
My dear swan, white as the clouds

never yet reaching them.
Insatiable instinct to fly reigns in feathers, beak
and curving neck—the desire to be.

Someday, you will learn to curve
your neck back towards your body,
catch and pull the wires between your beak.

Journey

He attempts to go back, my son,
to hear the continual thumping of a heartbeat.
That drumbeat beneath the melody of blood
rushing through arteries and the sounds of
muffled, but familiar voices coming from
some unknown world. The rain shushes like
the rush of amniotic fluid in the ear when he
could hear through water. So content to suck
on a finger, to wiggle and roll, weightless, being
rocked as I walked. He wraps himself in blankets,
curls up as if in a sac pressed against my inner belly.
And through the thin wall was a white light that
made me glow. How like a moth he rushes
into lamps. Each time, as if returning home, finally.

Truth is Black Rubber

Truth is Black Rubber

Smell of carbon black,
built under immense heat
and pressure.
Boys play with
the rubber doughnut
of the earth
through which they see
the sky, green mountains
and valleys.
Tire rolls down a hill.
A boy watches
its descent.

His friend sits on
the other tire, legs
on either side and waits,

both fixated on the rolling
as if all reality is in this moment
of a spinning rubber circle.

Inspired by H'mong kids in North Vietnam

Agent Orange

It's difficult to be alone, without
a mother's touch, in a crib like a
baby except one is not.

A son taught to live with a thirst
for a mother who loves her child though
one of his legs is too short, the other too long.

He sits, arms bent and limp, but do not
avoid him; he wants to interact. His swollen eyes
and misshapen head leans back. In a dream
Mother holds him close, as if by her embrace alone,
she will somehow right the wrong.

The chemical traveled through her placenta,
to the womb where small limbs that needed
to form couldn't, where the tiny body,
the size of a fist, no longer knew what to do.

It was named for the orange band
around each fifty-five gallon drum.

Orange as a sunrise that permeates one's soul,
how its rays cover the sky
and the earth with a deep orange,

rising as those bodies also rise.

Song of Massacre

*"I would say that most people in our company didn't con-
sider the Vietnamese human."*

—*Dennis Bunning, a U.S. Army
soldier during the My Lai Massacre*

On March 16, 1968—
the day etched into
my birth certificate
eight years later,
at the end of the war,
though not my real birthday.
500 deaths of unarmed
civilians. Women raped,
implosion of unwanted flesh
like unwavering knives and bullets.
Babies thrown to the ground.

Red stains the flag, stains the sky.
Stains the soil soaked
down to roots.

Life's liquid stains my heart red
on the day after
the Ides of March
and before St. Patrick's.

Death and shamrocks.

What it means to be human.

A Priori

Kangaroos

The distance between
the joey and the mother
is two feet.
The distance between
the joey and the mother
is forever
after she expels her baby
from the pouch
when chased by a predator.

Birds

The mother bird abandons
her nest after a suspected
disturbance.
A bird makes cost-deficit calculations—
risk death or leave her young.

Rats

A mother rat eats her whole
litter when stressed.
Then, she regains her energy.

Humans

A mother sells her child
in the hope of a better life
or for greed.

Water Buffalo
A village in Vietnam

One story:

Between 1975 to 1984,
my father, in "re-education"
camp, worked the job of
a thousand-pound water buffalo,
because he was considered an animal.

He pulled a plow, strapped
around his shoulders, trudging
knee-deep through rice fields.
With each step he took,
his foot sank and body became
heavy. The metal teeth of the plow
dug into the wet earth and Father pulled
as if he were carrying the entire mountain
of Hoang Lien Son.

This job was devoid of the games and laughter of children.
In the recesses of Father's mind was the faint
whisper of his son and daughter—so distant,
almost non-existent.

Another story:

When a droplet of sunrise
blends its colors into
the dark sky,
the workday begins.
An older child in the family,
knee-deep in water, tends
the water buffalo.
He brings the animal into
the rice fields to plow,
the tedious pull, muscles
in the body tense, softening the dirt
and mud below. Other children and women
bend over to plant rice seeds
into the holes and loosened soil.
In the late afternoon,
the small children
bring their water buffalos
to graze in the grasslands.

While their water buffalos
munch, the children
chase each other,
tell stories and laugh.

Then the children take
their water buffalos to a pond,
their bodies submerge in water,
their gentle heads gaze out.
The children, scrubbing and talking,
wash the water buffalos' bodies
with clean water.

Play mingles with work
and the children stand
on the backs of their
animals,
balancing and wobbling.
They yell, so the creatures
will move around.

At dusk, the children ride
their water buffalos home
in the receding sunlight, slow and
majestic. Their bare feet dangling
from the animals' sides, their bodies
tired, sore, and dirty from a day's
work, their hair wet.

On the children's mouths and
the water buffalos' backward
curving horns—
the nuance of a smile.

H'mong

A whole village
is blanketed
in the aerial spray
of chemical genocide.

Soft clouds cover
mountaintops.

~

In a field, a grandmother
carries her grandchild
in a pouch on her back
as she works.
Their heartbeats
synchronize.

~

People who are connected
to the earth, know its secrets –
medicinal, weather, plants for dyeing.

~

A woman is sewing.
Between her fingers,
the needle dives into cloth
and emerges, pulling along
colored patterns, stories
and customs into handmade
clothing.

~

H'mong is a word
that means "freedom."
It is difficult to cross
the Mekong River
to a refugee camp
without getting killed.

How many dead flowers are scattered about the land?

Saigon
1995

A pearl in my hand.
I was born in this "Paris" of buildings
and monuments, of war remnants,

of flags that stand side-by-side in the street,
of motorbikes that circle and circle,
drawing rings of light into the dark night.

Air thick with exhaust, fumes,
a greasy film covers the face.

Black-and-white clouds of ash and polluted
air hang above. City of barefoot children,
of bright, yellow sunlight that makes

a woman's dress stick to her skin.
City of apartments that look
as if a strong wind could blow them
over into the sandy streets.
Sheets cover openings in walls.
People sell food and knick-knacks

on the street under apartments.
Conversations and engines fill ears.

City of pho, of Buddhist temples,
of children who beg with bowl in hands.
This falling, a heart's tearing

from branch to soil, the turning leaf
flutters in the breeze in a slight confusion
of where it should be.

I am drawn to grass,
to fields and forests, mountains, sunsets
and cities, skies that I have seen in dreams,

to twigs from which this city is named.

Photosynthesis

Cashews

Edible moon
Two crescents stuck together
Though the moon outside
Is whole and blue! Tonight
I have my half circles
Little, tasty smiles
On New Year's Eve

A swing's upward path
Held between my index finger
And thumb

A small boat on the lake
Of my tongue

Disappears one by one

Above—a full moon
Made of a cashew
Split into two

Maps

Pieces of broken crackers—the geometry of the United States.
Your finger traces a blue highway along the Atlantic coast and
    pauses at periods.
I seek out circled stars on a page and name them,
find vast open green spaces and cities within a centimeter of
    white paper—
to journey back in time and hear stories.
My hand lifts an entire state and turns it over
to where it continues on the other side.
I lie here on your bed looking at maps
thinking—*Travel me, enter my capital.*
Your heart—a matrix,
womb from where
everything grows.

Intimacy

The sky is the color of hydrangea;
blanched clouds and shades of purple-blue,
a touch of pink-flushed petals here and there.
Hydrangea in morning sun and afternoon shade
where thoughts like winged insects alight
on a cluster of forty-three blossoms—
blossoms that color according to the aluminum
or lack of the metal in the soil.

How Chopsticks Were Invented

Against a backdrop of sunset,
two reed-like legs are dipped into water.
Snake-like neck swings back
then forward like a sword
and catches a small fish
between its beak.

Anyone who folds a thousand cranes
will receive their heart's desire.
At the table, a woman's arm
is a neck in its loose white sleeve.
Rice, chicken, broccoli carried
on the tip of chopsticks.

Bike Accident

My closest encounter with a rose
bush was when I crashed into one.
While a child and riding my bike,
I thought I would challenge myself—
pedal fast, let go of my feet and hands.
Then, I lost control and went straight into
a rose bush. The bike on top of me, thorns
in my body. Flesh cut and bleeding.
The rose entered my bloodstream
and eyelids scattered over me.

I guess it was then, as when Peter Parker was
bitten by a spider and became Spiderman—when I became a poet.

Resourcefulness
Santa Catalina Island in Soloman Islands Archipelago

The fisherman finds a strong spider web,
wraps the silk around a stick.
He paddles out in a wooden boat
to catch needle fish,
the fish that can't be caught with a hook,
because its mouth is too narrow.
For centuries this is how it is done.
In the waters, he takes out a small, black kite,
slips the wound web off the stick,
and ties the kite string around it.
The wind carries the kite up into the sky.
The glob of web bobs like an insect across the water.
The fisherman holds the kite's string in his mouth.
When the kite drops, the fish is ensnared;
its sharp teeth and rough scales are trapped in the web.
And the fisherman slowly pulls the string towards himself.
The needle fish moves its hips and swims in the clear water.
The fisherman lifts the fish up,
flickering for a moment in the sunlight.
He holds it gently in his hand,
placing the narrow mouth of the fish
in his mouth sideways and slides off the web.
He places the fish next to the pile of fish
on the boat's floor.

L'art D'aimer
from the perspective of Baltimore Orioles

First are the songs— a composition of whistles
and rattles. *You always hear an oriole before
you see one.* Then copulation; black and
orange ruffles in leaves. They find a branch high
above the ground to weave a bag. Pieces of plastic strips,
strings, branches, grass, one by one in the beak,
mixes with saliva. In the building and in its intent
is nest and what is to come afterwards—eggs,
hatchlings helpless and blind, throats stretched
out in a chorale for food. Insect legs dangle
from a parent's beak. The younglings will soon leave
the nest with a nudge off the edge—the first time
wings are used to convince air of its ability.
Between two elm trunks vertical and black—
bird in sky is an absolute.

Chinese Female Kung-Fu Superheroes

are real. They jump from roof-top
to roof-top, do a backward flip
down to the concrete floor and land
perfectly on two feet.

The metal of swords clang,
the body moves with the precision
of a praying mantis striking
its prey.

Their dresses are colorful, long
and lacy, billow and flair
with each turn and twist.

Jewelry in the hair dangles and sparkles.

Chinese female kung-fu superheroes
are smart, fight bad guys, do good deeds,
and risk their lives.
They appear when least expected.

Chinese female kung-fu superheroes
never give up. They travel often alone
by foot through mountains. They work hard
training to master various martial arts forms.

They do not care about Barbies,
those plastic dolls of only one hair color
that just looked pretty in the 80's. They aren't
impressed; they do not want a boring life.

Chinese female kung-fu superheroes venture out
and save cities against villains. They steal into the night
in their black ninja-like suits, soundlessly through a house
to recover a magical sword and to release a prisoner,
knowing exactly where to press with their two fingertips
to freeze the guards and to accomplish their mission.

After Jeannine Hall Gailey's
Becoming the Villainess

The Unknown Woman

As she washes the grains of rice,
stirs the embers for fire
for the soup in the stone pot cooking,
she ponders words and sounds
and feelings.
She writes poems in the wind,
in the soil,
in the clouds.
The words sweep back
and forth with the bamboo
broom with grass bristles,
go up in plumes
with the chicken feathered duster.
As she carries the water from the river,
and washes the clothes,
the words swoosh, swoosh,
back and forth, back and forth.
In her mind, sway,
never really going anywhere.
At night, as she removes the intricate
flower-shaped pin from her hair,
all the poems tumble down.
As she closes her eyes
for the night, gathered
around her arms,
verses soft as her silk robe
pressed next to her quietly singing
heart.
Moonlight in the night,
a glow in her dark eyes
behind a curtain of skin.

Newton's First Law of Motion

An object is in a state of inertia, that is, a kind of constant motion, until another force interferes with its course, like when my state of mind is rattled. Sometimes the force appears as a person, an object or feeling. Sometimes it comes flying from a distance—a firebird. Winged creature, Feng Huang, of luck and happiness with the tail of a fish, the head of a cock, the back of a swallow, and the neck of a snake, that plunges into fire and turns into ashes—strange, mythical bird that never dies. It is because you die and die and return each time, it is because in order to be reborn, you must die. And so people wear jeweled phoenixes of jade and gemstone around their necks and wrists and embroider the firebird into a piece of art to place on the wall. They play the five notes of your song, the notes of the pentatonic scale, because of its magical powers. I want to be you, Ho-o, and cast myself into the fire again and again. Keep my heart open and burning, allow something to fly in and a new bird to soar from my chest.

Photosynthesis
  for my son

How can I convince you
that you do have chlorophyll,
that you can take the sun's
energy and turn it into sugar?
Produce something sweet inside of you.
Take the waste people breathe out
and make it into something that
will keep you alive, that will keep
those around you alive, create oxygen.

Why do you say that this metaphor
doesn't work, that you don't have
the powers of a plant, that nature
didn't intend you that way?

Look, how you twist and turn
towards the light.

Untitled Space

Newton's First, Second, and Third Laws of Motion

> *"Every object in a state of uniform motion tends to remain in that state of motion unless an external force is applied to it."*
>
> *"The relationship between an object's mass m, its acceleration a, and the applied force F is F = ma."*
>
> *"For every action, there is an opposite and equal reaction."*

There are different kinds of war.

Two people push each other, shoulder to shoulder, exert force—then a punch, a kick.

A tug of war—hands clenched, pulling, the weight tips to one end, then to the other. Each side wants to possess the other.

Death does not discriminate—two people fall at the same speed of 9.8 meters per second squared.

Bombs have the force to destroy whole cities and incinerate whole peoples or separate their limbs—an arm flies here and a leg flies there, the heart splatters somewhere.

Nerve gases, though banned, are still used. They choke the victim from the inside, it is a slow death.

When a sharp, metal object enters the body with weight and acceleration, the force will tear the body open and puncture bone, organ. Blood will flow out of the body in its own motion.

The force of a bullet is its speed, about 1000 meters per second, times its mass. A bullet's aim is direct—it has only two purposes—kill or seriously injure.

In war, there is ambush.

A human body will stop the path of a bullet.

Once a war begins, it is never really over. Families and loved ones mourn. A war's force is present through the years, after decades, centuries. It is something that lingers in the air.

Protest is good—a war for freedom and liberty. A peaceful war like Gandhi's.

Putting the guns down is friction. It will slow the war down until it seems like there is no war, but $F = ma$. The effect of war continues, long after it is over, in ever-expanding waves.

Playground

"Happiness is a ball after which we run wherever it rolls,
and we push it with our feet when it stops."
  —*Johann Wolfgang von Goethe*

The tank was the color of desert sand,
it rolled by like a slow-moving beetle
and dropped a glove gently to the ground.
The glove was a baseball glove.
A few boys huddled around
and one of them picked it up.
Inside the glove was a metal ball. A glove and a ball.
Another boy suggested taking the ball apart
and selling the metal pieces.
The boys began to hammer it.
One of the boys held the ball in his hand
and threw it against the wall.
The ball bounced back and exploded in his abdomen.
The dead boy was brought to the morgue.
Women gathered to identify the mutilated body.
The boys who survived walked around with furrowed brows
and a deep silence that only such shock could induce
surrounded by wails—a room full of people without furniture,
drowning in a sea of sand, sand they had believed held water.

Eternity in Gaza
Khan Younis Refugee Camp, 2001

When the canisters fell, they were ready,
thinking, "More tear gas," but a white cloud
flowered above, then changed colors and emitted
a sweet odor that made them want to breathe in
the way one breathes in the smell of sweet tea.

The color darkened until it looked like a burning
and people ran to put out what they thought were
fires on their neighbors' rooftops. Muscles began to
cramp, constricting as if from the bite of a scorpion.
A woman dropped her child as she scratched herself in a fit

of convulsions. A father attempted to hold down
his son who flailed and moaned until he fell into a coma.
The teenagers who played with the canisters, who taunted
their apparent harmlessness, shrieked and shook in pain for weeks.
The doctors had never seen anything like this before. The villagers

had never seen anything like this before. The convulsions came
like waves for an entire month and family members who sat and
    cried at bedside
wailed in pain almost as much as the victims who looked like
    rabid dogs.
Some visitors were stunned silent, their eyes inward, heads tilted
    to the side
as if not looking would somehow make it not be truly happening.

In a laboratory far away were beakers, scientists in white gowns
    and goggles,
microscopes, and gloves. At the end of the day, they went home
to their wives and wives to their husbands. The tables were set,
the dinner was ready, warm and steaming,
and the children swung their legs beneath the table.

Cam On

I wanted to learn so many
languages: Latin, Spanish,
German, Hebrew, Russian,
Chinese, Korean, and Japanese.
These languages moved me
with their music and passion.
I hated to hear Vietnamese.
It sounded ugly; I did not
even want to look at the words
in print.

All I could see were people running,
hiding in trenches.
All I could hear were anxious voices.
I did not see the words, I could
not hear the words.

Now, something is changing:

I *want* to learn to speak the language
of the country where I was born,
no longer spinning.

Xin chao—hello

Cam on—thank you

How the song of the gong
is summoning me back.

Fractures

I cannot open the book
or read the words in
Vietnamese, because it opens
up history;
the child afraid of the violent
stranger.

Even when the words
have nothing to do with war.
Perhaps it's the shape or sound
from each letter, the accents.

There is a village when I read
the words, there are guns held
up towards a target and doors
kicked open, the way a language
enters a body without consent.

How can I allow sound
into my body?

Let language enter without pain,
without shaking with fear.

Tell myself it's okay, open, open.

Napalm and all the variations of the name still being used

"The communication of the dead is tongued with fire beyond the language of the living."

—*T.S. Eliot*

The best containers
for fire are made of metal,
glas or stone.
But this fire is too hot,
too large,
too targeted
to be contained.
It was made to spread wildly,
to stick itself onto human skin,
sear tissues, muscles, organs.
This fire was made
to burn people alive.

This fire was not made
to be put out.

I spread my heart
over half a century,
across thousands of miles
and many countries,

over the victims
burned, ashes, and still burning,
over white phosphorous,
carbon monoxide.

Let my heart hold this bomb,
Let my arteries and capillaries
wrap around it, keep it in place.

Rough Draft

The word, though spelled incorrectly, is mine. I cross it out in my own time and in its space, the brown earth, I will grow flowers, fruit trees, or lettuce. I am a rough draft, cursive drawn on paper with a pen and my left hand rubs over the ink. The blue smears the way water bleeds. My thoughts color the white space with curving lines, see how they keep moving like whiskered catfish. Words move over other words, along the top, a caret fills in what was left out. I cross out a word that doesn't sound right and replace it with another—my words have larynx, are string. There are paragraphs I wish I could delete but I don't and I can't; rough drafts are made, the way we can't erase the past. I am adding and simplifying. I come from ancestors who are herbal doctors, how they mix plants and seeds and barks and roots, the way I mix words to create a horrid tasting black liquid that is good for the health. I want to take grammar and break it up and put them together again like lego pieces and build something else, anything else, perhaps a bird. I am a constant participial phrase. The appositive does not define me though it tries to. My hair is too long? Should I cut it? I will proofread. No, I will not cut it. Let the blank spaces cuddle the words and let my hair grow long as the lines from my pen, how they draw and draw lines fine and dark as my hair. I carry a dictionary in my arms. My body is a rough draft; in my blood, the letters float like cells. I need to go for walks, separate these words, let each be round, infused with oxygen. I will never be a final draft. I will never be done, complete in my journal I hide under the bed—it is not meant to be proofread.

What Was and What Will Be
"Beauty awaits in ambush for us."
                    —Jorge Luis Borges

It wasn't the flu, it wasn't the flu.
There wasn't anything she could do
to protect her child
from something so silent
and invisible and violent.

The universe works in strange ways.
How could Staph just invade
and take a fetus from its
mother's belly in a flash?

One day, the robin in the black ash
will startle me with its song.
I am wrong, nature again will win
the argument.

When I First Saw Daddy

he was like an Egyptian cat;
skinny, foraging, and stern,
just released from a Vietcong prison.
He told us he hated the color red.
Sixteen years later,
he wears a red sweatshirt and smiles.
The pin tip opening in his heart enough
to let in a driblet of red.

Devotion

My mother crushes
a fly between
her hands.

She does so with
such precision
and calculation.

Just one clap
and the fly is dead.

My mother prays
to Buddha every day,

lights the sticks of incense
and places them
next to each god and goddess.

She always mentions our names
in her prayers.

My mother is full of compassion
and love even as the fly

is squashed between her hands.

In Praise of Emptiness

I am looking for what's not there:
that space we look through,
the curve of a bowl,
a window.
Blankness on paper:
the smooth white
between words,
between lines,
what is not said,
what is not done.
The hollow in a bird's bones.

When someone looks at my palms,
it's as if I'm holding nothing
but the world.

Vietnamese Globe

In Vietnamese, the word "to live"
is a circle. A question mark rests
at the top and a comma to the right
of the question. Except, the question
mark has no dot at the bottom,
so the curve is like the curve of a cane
where the hand grips

or a squiggle of hair from the head.
It is a beautiful word—a
painting. Round as a ball
and at the summit of this *living*,
one wonders and pauses.

The earth is shaped like this word, circling.
Cycling—carbon, phosphorous, nitrogen,
water, sediments.
A bird with a worm wiggling from its
beak will eventually become Origin.

My mouth opens wide and spherical
to sound this Vietnamese globe—

"Eoehh"

ACKNOWLEDGMENTS

Grateful acknowledgment is made to the editors of the following publications in which these poems previously appeared, sometimes in different form:

CHAPBOOKS
Cartesian Product (Silkworms Ink, 2010): "Immigration," "Cock-roaches," "Welding," "Vietnam Ghost Stories," "Hut-yee," "A Story of Mother and Daughter," "Cartesian Product," "Hugging My Grand-ma," "Rose," "Cam On"
Cartography of Family (Chippens Press, 2010): "The Bomb Shelter," "Not Worth a Bullet," "Journey," "Moon Festival," "When I First Saw Daddy"
Danaus Plexippus Plexippus (Victorian Violet Press, 2010): "Intimacy," "How Chopsticks were Invented," "Bike Accident," "Resourceful-ness," "L'art D'aimer," "Cashews," "Maps"
Truth is Black Rubber (Silkworms Ink, 2010): "Truth is Black Rubber," "Agent Orange," "Song of Massacre," "Wired Swan," "A Priori," "Water Buffalo," "H'mong," "Saigon," "Vietnamese Globe," "Chinese Female Kung-Fu Superheroes," "Grandma (A Hologram)"

ANTHOLOGY
L (Silkworms Ink, 2011): "Eternity in Gaza"

JOURNALS
Ascent Aspirations Magazine: "Cashews"
Community Life Magazine (Monroe County, Ohio): "When I First Saw Daddy"
Da Mau Literary Magazine: "When I First Saw Daddy," "Not Worth a Bullet," "Moon Festival" (translated into Vietnamese by Le Dinh Nhat Lang)
EarthSpeak Magazine: "Photosynthesis"
Miller's Pond: "Maps"
The National Poetry Review: "L'art D'aimer"
Pitkin Review: "Newton's First, Second, and Third Laws of Motion"
The Prose-Poem Project: "Newton's First Law of Motion"
Rattle: "Playground"
Saltwater Quarterly: "Quantum Equation"
The Splinter Generation: "Rough Draft"
Urban Confusions: "Quantum Equation," "Vietnamese Globe," "Chinese Female Kung-Fu Superheroes"
Verse Daily: "L'art D'aimer"

I would like to thank my family, friends, and mentors for their gener-ous support, encouragement, and inspiration.